JEWISH
Prayer and Worship

Jonathan Gorsky and Anita Ganeri

W
FRANKLIN WATTS
LONDON•SYDNEY

First published in 2006 by
Franklin Watts
338 Euston Road
London NW1 3BH

Franklin Watts Australia
Hachette Children's Books
Level 17/207 Kent Street
Sydney NSW2000

Editor: Rachel Cooke
Design: Joelle Wheelwright
Picture researcher: Diana Morris
Acknowledgements: David Bartruff/Corbis: front cover b. Wendy
Connett/Alamy: 5. Chris Fairclough/Franklin Watts: 7, 9, 26. Itzhak
Genut/Ark Religion: 14. Mark E. Gibson/Corbis: 20. Roger Hutchings/
Alamy: 27. Hutchison/Eye Ubiquitous: front cover c. Jenny Matthews/
Franklin Watts: 15, 16, 21. Richard Nowitz/Israel Images: 23. James
Nubile/Image Works/Topfoto: 6, 18. Eyal Ofer/Corbis: 22. Picturepoint/
Topfoto: 17. Roger Ressmeyer/Corbis: 28. Rex Features: 11. Helene
Rogers/Ark Religion: 25. Steve Shott/Franklin Watts: 8, 12. Topfoto:
10, 29. Adina Tovy/Ark Religion: 24. David H Wells/Corbis: 13.

A CIP catalogue record for this book is available
from the British Library.

Dewey Decimal Classification Number: 296

ISBN-10: 0 7496 5936 X
ISBN-13: 978 0 7496 5936 3

Printed in China

Contents

The prayers in this book were chosen by Jonathan Gorsky. Jonathan is Education Advisor for the Council of Christians and Jews. He is an historian who spent a number of years in rabbinic study and was previously Education Director of a Jewish centre for adult education. He has a particular interest in modern Jewish spirituality.

About Judaism

Judaism is the religion of the Jewish people. Anyone born of a Jewish mother is considered to be a Jew, even if they do not actively practise their religion. According to the Torah (the Jewish holy book), God chose a man called Abraham to be the father of the Jews. Abraham was the leader of a group of nomadic people, called the Hebrews, who lived in the Middle East some 4,000 years ago.

The Star of David is a symbol of the Jewish religion. David was a Jewish king who is famous for writing psalms.

Jewish beliefs

Jews believe in one God who created the world and continues to work in the world, affecting everything that people do. They believe that God made a covenant (agreement) with Abraham. God promised to guide and care for the Jews, if the Jews kept the laws which God had given to them, loved God and led holy lives. The Jews believe that they were chosen by God to set an example of holiness in the world.

4

Even if our songs were like the waters of the ocean
And our tongues were as joyful as the waves of the sea,
If our praise filled the heavens,
If our faces shone like the sun and moon,
If our hands were to hover in the sky like eagles,
If our feet could run across mountains as swiftly as deer,
All that would not be enough to thank You,
O Lord my God.

About this prayer
This joyful prayer was composed over 1,500 years ago. Jews often sing it in the synagogue on Shabbat and during some festivals. When Jews sing this prayer, they think of the Earth, the heavens and the vast universe. Later, they stand in silence and pray. They know that they cannot begin to understand God who created the world, and turn from words of praise to quiet contemplation. They know that they are in the presence of holiness that words cannot describe or understand.

Jews around the world

Today, there are about 15 million Jews. They live all over the world but mostly in Israel, the USA and Europe. For many Jews, Israel is the land promised to them by God long ago. Orthodox Jews follow all the traditions and laws of Judaism, many of which are more than 2,000 years old. Progressive Jews believe that these traditions must be adapted to suit the needs of the modern world. This book contains prayers and images from both branches.

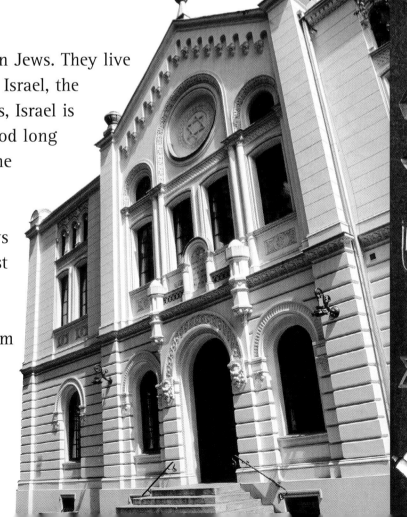

This is the Nozyk synagogue which serves the Jewish community in Warsaw, Poland.

5

Jewish Prayer and Worship

Prayer is very important in the Jewish religion. For Jews, praying is a way of communicating with God and of spending time with God. In the hustle and bustle of everyday life, prayer helps Jews to remember the holiness of life, and the preciousness of all creation.

Jews pray together in a synagogue in Romania.

Saying prayers

Many Jews pray three times a day - in the morning, afternoon and evening. They also say shorter prayers, called blessings, at other times. Prayers may be said at home but many Jews like to visit the synagogue to pray with others. Some prayers praise or thank God for his kindness and care. Others remind people of how God wants them to live. Prayers may be said or sung but the holiest prayers are recited while standing quietly. Whenever and wherever prayers are said, the most important thing is that they come from the heart.

Language of prayer

Many prayers are said in Hebrew, the ancient language of the Jews. The Torah (see pages 8–9) is written in Hebrew, and many Jewish children learn Hebrew from an early age. But prayers can be said in any language because Jews believe that God can understand them, whichever language is being spoken.

Jewish prayer book

The Jewish prayer book is called the Siddur. It is a collection of psalms, blessings, passages from the Torah and prayers written by early rabbis. In Hebrew, the word 'Siddur' means 'order', and the book gives the set order in which daily prayers should be said. Services in the synagogue follow this order. This means Jews can join in the prayers wherever they are in the world.

Here a Siddur (Jewish prayer book), rests on a prayer shawl.

I will lift my eyes unto the hills,
From where my help will come.
My help comes from the Lord,
Who made heaven and Earth.
He will make sure your foot
does not stumble.
He that looks after you will
not slumber.
He that guards Israel
Will neither slumber nor sleep.

About this prayer

In addition to the set prayers, Jews also sometimes say personal prayers. But many turn to songs called psalms instead. These are found in the Book of Psalms in the Hebrew Bible. They help Jews to express their deep feelings in times of joy or sorrow. This prayer is an extract from Psalm 121. It is recited as a prayer by people and communities in times of distress. It reassures Jews that God will always support them.

7

Holy Books

Many Jewish prayers, and passages used in worship, come from the Torah, the most important part of the Jewish scriptures. The Torah is made up of the first five books of the Tenakh, or Hebrew Bible. Other prayers come from other books of the Bible, such as the Book of Psalms (see page 7). Some of the most important prayers were written by rabbis and other great religious teachers, and most are very ancient.

↑ *The Torah scrolls are the focal point of a synagogue and are kept in a special alcove, called the Ark.*

The Torah

The five books of the Torah (which means teaching) are also called the Five Books of Moses. They are Genesis, Exodus, Leviticus, Numbers and Deuteronomy. Jews believe that God spoke the Torah to Moses and that Moses wrote the words down. The Torah contains many stories about the first Jews, and many rules about how Jews should live. The best-known of these are the Ten Commandments. For Jews, the text of the Torah is their link with God. It is read on Shabbat (see pages 14–17), festivals and at some weekday services.

Sacred scrolls

The words of the Torah are hand-written on scrolls. These scrolls are the most precious possessions of any Jewish community. They are wrapped in velvet mantles (covers) and kept in the Ark, a special alcove at the front of the synagogue. When the scrolls are taken out of the Ark, they are paraded around the synagogue while prayers are sung. People bow as the scrolls pass, or kiss the corner of the mantles with their prayer shawls (see page 13).

A Progressive rabbi reads from the Torah scroll. She uses a yad (pointer) to avoid touching the sacred scroll.

*With everlasting love, You have loved Your people, the House of Israel.
You have taught us Torah and commandments, laws and judgements.
Therefore, O Lord our God, we will speak of Your laws
When we lie down and when we rise up,
Rejoicing in the words of Your Torah and Your commandments for ever.
For they are our life and the length of our days;
We will meditate on them day and night.
May You never take away Your love from us.
Blessed are You, O Lord, who loves His people Israel.*

About this prayer

This ancient prayer is said in the evenings. It expresses the great sense of love Jews feel for the Torah. It reminds them of the importance of the commandments and laws God has given them. The prayer also recognises how, by reading and studying the Torah, Jews feel closer to God and His love.

Worship in the Synagogue

Many Jews visit a synagogue to worship. Praying with other people is an important way of showing that they are part of their own Jewish community and of the community of Jews all over the world. But a synagogue is not only a place for prayer and worship. It is also the centre of Jewish community life and a place for learning more about Judaism.

Inside a synagogue

At the front of the synagogue is the Ark (see page 9). A light, called the Ner Tamid (Eternal Light) always burns above it as a symbol of God's presence. In front of the Ark is the Bimah (a raised platform) where the Torah scrolls are placed to be read. When Jews pray, they face the front of the synagogue. This is so that they face in the direction of the holy city of Jerusalem.

Inside a synagogue. The Ark is in the alcove at the centre of the photograph, with the Bimah in front of it. In Orthodox synagogues, like this one, women sit in galleries, apart from the men.

↑ *A rabbi gives a talk at a service.*

Synagogue services

Services are held every day in the synagogue, in the morning, afternoon and evening. The most important service is on Shabbat morning (Saturday). Weekday services may last for about half an hour but services are longer on Shabbat and festival days. Services include prayers, psalms, hymns and readings from the Torah. They may be led by a rabbi, a cantor, or a member of the congregation. The rabbi may also give a talk about that week's Torah reading.

Lord, open my lips and my mouth shall declare Your praise.

Blessed are You, Lord our God, and God of our fathers, God of Abraham, God of Isaac, and God of Jacob, the great, the mighty, and the awesome God, God beyond, generous in love and kindness, and possessing all. He remembers the good deeds of our fathers, and therefore in love brings rescue to the generations, for such is His being. He is the king who helps and saves and shields. Blessed are You Lord, the shield of Abraham.

About this prayer

This is the first blessing from the Amida, one of the holiest Jewish prayers. It focuses on Abraham, Isaac and Jacob, the fathers of the Jewish people, and on God's relationship with them. The Amida is a series of blessings. There are 19 blessings on weekdays, and seven for Shabbat and festivals. The word 'Amida' means 'standing' in Hebrew. Before the prayer begins, Jews take three steps forward as if approaching God. Then they stand with their feet together, bowing several times during the prayer. When the prayer is finished, they take three steps back. The prayer is said very quietly, with great respect and reverence.

Showing respect

At services in the synagogue, Jewish men, boys and married women cover their heads when they pray, as a sign of respect to God. Some men wear a small, round cap, called a kippah. Others wear an ordinary hat because they believe that their whole heads should be covered. In Progressive synagogues, some women also wear kippot.

A Jewish boy wearing a kippah holds up the Torah after reading from it.

And it shall come to pass, if you listen to my commandments which I give you this day, to love the Lord your God, and to serve Him with all your heart and with all your soul, that I will send you rain for your land so that you can have corn, wine and oil. And I will send grass for your fields, so that you can eat and be full. But take care that your heart does not turn away from God.
(Deuteronomy 11: 13-16)

And so it shall be as a sign upon your hand and as a symbol on your forehead that with a mighty hand the Lord freed us from Egypt.
(Exodus 13: 9)

About these passages

These two passages are from the four extracts from the Torah which are placed inside tefillin (see right). The first section is also recited as part of the Shema prayer (see page 18). Like the passage given from Exodus, all four extracts contain the instruction to wear tefillin. When Jews bind on the tefillin, they feel like they are tying themselves close to God. They remember the generous gifts He gives them, from the food on their table to freedom from slavery.

Clothes for prayer

At morning services, some Jews wear a tallit (prayer shawl). They wrap it around their shoulders to show that God is all around them. A tallit is usually made of white or cream silk or wool, with blue or black stripes. The fringes at the edges remind the wearer to follow God's commandments which are found in the Torah.

Some Jews wear two small leather boxes, called tefillin, during prayers. Each box has a leather strap. One box is tied to the forehead; the other to the upper arm, facing the heart. Inside are tiny scrolls on which are written four passages from the Torah (see left). Wearing tefillin is a reminder to love God with all the heart and with all the mind. The tefillin are always treated with great care and respect.

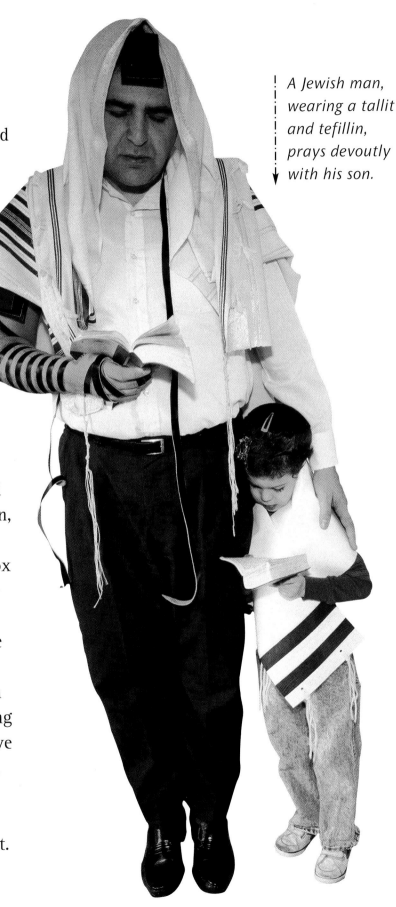

A Jewish man, wearing a tallit and tefillin, prays devoutly with his son.

13

Shabbat Prayers at Home

Jews often worship at home. Family worship is important for Jews. It helps them to feel a close bond with Jews all over the world. The most important day of the week is Shabbat, the Jewish day of rest and prayer. On Shabbat, Jews remember how God rested after creating the world. There are also special Shabbat services in the synagogue (see page 11).

Day of rest

The Torah instructs Jews to rest on Shabbat. Some Jews follow this rule very closely. They do not work, go shopping, or drive their cars. They prepare all their food the day before. Some will not even watch television. Other Jews are less strict. Jews believe that Shabbat is part of the covenant between God and the Jewish people. They see it as a gift from God. It is a time when they do not make use of the world as they would during the week, but remember and celebrate the holiness of creation.

A Jewish family gather together to celebrate Shabbat.

↑ *A Jewish mother prepares to light the Shabbat candles.*

Shabbat begins

Shabbat lasts from just before sunset on Friday afternoon to Saturday night. On Friday, the house is cleaned and the table set. At dusk, the mother of the family lights two candles to welcome Shabbat. Everyone then goes to the synagogue and returns home for the Shabbat meal.

Our God and God of our fathers, accept our rest. Give us through Your commandments, a sense of the holy And let us share in the knowledge of Your Word. Fill us with Your goodness, Make us joyful with Your help. Cleanse our hearts to serve You truly. Through Your love and grace, O Lord our God, Make Your holy Shabbat become our own; May Israel rest that day and praise Your name.

About this prayer

This prayer is part of the Amida, which is said during the various Shabbat services in the synagogue. The Amida is said quietly by everyone and then recited out loud by the person leading the service. Jews believe God's commandments are His way of telling them what He wants them to do. They are accepted with love and give Jews a sense of God's holiness and how close He is to them at all times.

The Shabbat meal

The Shabbat meal is a time for the family to come together and to think about God. The meal always includes two loaves of special bread, called challah. They remind Jews of when their ancestors wandered through the desert after their escape from slavery in Egypt. On Friday, God sent them two loaves of bread so that they did not have to bake on Saturday.

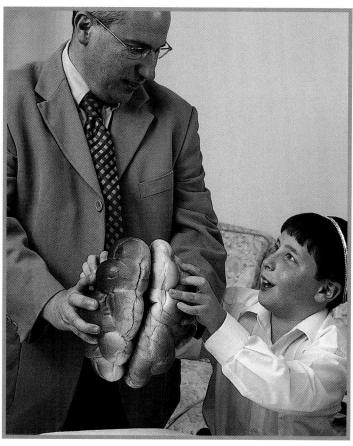

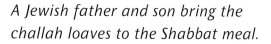

A Jewish father and son bring the challah loaves to the Shabbat meal.

Blessed are You, O Lord our God,
King of the Universe,
Who created the fruits of the vine.
Blessed are You, O Lord,
Who made us holy with Your commandments
And in Your love gave us the Sabbath day
In remembrance of Your creation.
It is the most important of all our holy days,
Recalling the exodus from slavery in Egypt,
Because You chose us out of all the peoples
And in Your love gave us the gift
Of this holy day.
Blessed are You, O Lord, who made the
Sabbath holy.

About this prayer
This prayer is the blessing called the Kiddush. Before the Shabbat meal begins, the family stand at their places around the table, and a glass of wine or grape juice is poured for everyone. Then one person, usually the father or mother, raises his or her glass of wine and recites the Kiddush blessing to make the Shabbat holy.

End of Shabbat

To mark the end of Shabbat, a farewell ceremony is held after nightfall on Saturday. This is called Havdalah which means 'separation'. Blessings are recited over a glass of wine, a box of sweet-smelling spices and a special candle which is plaited and has two wicks. After the spices blessing, everyone sniffs to carry the sweetness of Shabbat with them into the rest of the week. The ceremony ends with the Havdalah blessing which separates the holy Shabbat day from the rest of the week. Everyone has a sip of wine and some wine is spilled into a saucer and used to put the candle out. This symbolises the restful influence of Shabbat spilling out into the working week.

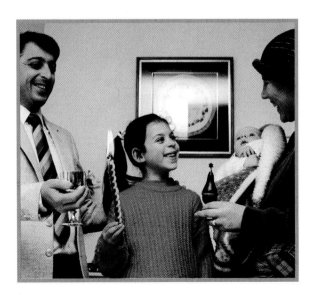

↑ *A Jewish family celebrate*
¡ *Havdalah at the end of Shabbat.*

God of Abraham, of Isaac,
and of Jacob,
Protect Your dear people of Israel
with Your love.

The good and holy
Shabbat nears its end,
Now turn to us in tenderness,
and send
A happy week, abrim
With life and health,
with bread and savour.
Let us be pure and righteous,
grant us Thy favour,
Untarnished gains and greater
strength of limb.

Elijah, the prophet, is in our house,
All evil things shall keep out,
All good shall enter by this door
And never leave us any more.

About this prayer

This folk-prayer from Eastern Europe is sung after Havdalah. It asks for protection in the coming week and that people may be happy, healthy and successful. Elijah is a biblical prophet who, according to Jewish tradition, still appears among people in times of need to look after and support them.

Morning and Evening Prayers

There are many Jewish prayers which may be said in the mornings and evenings. Beginning the day with prayer is a way of giving thanks to God for our waking up and being alive. Ending the day with prayer is a way of thanking God for the day that has passed and of asking for His protection during the night ahead.

Jews saying the Shema prayer in the morning.

Hear O Israel, the Lord is our God, the Lord is One.
Blessed is His name, whose glorious kingdom is forever and ever.
Love your Lord with all your heart, and all your soul, and all your might. These words that I command you today shall be upon your heart. Repeat them to your children, and talk about them when you sit in your home, and when you walk in the street; when you lie down, and when you rise up.
Hold fast to them as a sign upon your hand, and let them be reminders before your eyes. Write them on the doorposts of your home and at your gates.

About this prayer

This is the first verse of the Shema, one of the holiest Jewish prayers. The word 'Shema' means 'hear'. This prayer is said every morning and evening, and is the first prayer which Jewish children learn. Apart from the second line, it comes from the Torah. Many different aspects of Jewish religious life are expressed through the prayer – faith, love, study and practice – and it is said with great reverence. Jews cover their eyes when they say the first line as if they were actually able to see before them the holiness of God's presence.

Night-time prayers

Jews believe that before you go to sleep at night, your mind should be calm and peaceful. Some Jews take time before they sleep to go back over the events of the day. Apart from the Shema, Jews may say a prayer to ask for forgiveness if they have hurt someone's feelings, or to forgive someone who has offended them. They also pray for God's protection.

A Jewish child prays before going to sleep.

Within His hand I lay my soul
Both when I sleep and
when I wake,
And with my soul my body too,
My Lord is close,
I shall not fear.

About this prayer
Before going to sleep, some Jewish children may say a prayer like this one. Through this prayer, they ask God to protect them and keep them safe during the night. They will probably have learnt this prayer and the Shema by heart.

Daily Blessings

Many Jews say short prayers called blessings as they go about their daily activities. They recite blessings over things they eat, see, smell, hear and so on. There are blessings for every occasion, from eating a meal, to starting a journey, to hearing the sound of thunder.

Jews may say a blessing when they see a tree in blossom.

After a meal
Blessed be our God, of whose gifts we have eaten
And by whose goodness we live.

Before a journey
May it be Your Will, Eternal God, to guide me
in peace and direct my steps so as to keep
me safe from all dangers along the way, and
bring blessing to the work of my hands, and
to bring me home in peace.

On hearing thunder
Blessed are You, Source of all Life,
filling the world with power and might.

For trees blossoming
Blessed are You, Source of all Life,
Whose world lacks nothing, creating
Goodly trees for our enjoyment.

About these prayers
These blessings are at least 1,800 years old and come from the ancient writings of Jewish rabbis. They are said aloud by adults and children alike. When someone recites a blessing, those who hear it say 'Amen' when it is finished. 'Amen' means 'So be it' in Hebrew. This shows that the listeners share the faith that the blessing has expressed.

Saying a blessing

In Judaism, there are blessings for every sort of food and every occasion in life. Saying a blessing is a way of giving thanks to God, and of showing that God is involved in everything Jews do. Blessings remind Jews that God is present at all times in their lives, not just on special or holy occasions.

Fixing a mezuzah

A mezuzah is a small case which Jews fix to the doorposts of their homes. The box contains a tiny piece of parchment on which is written parts of the Shema prayer (see page 18). The words command Jews to fix a mezuzah to

On fixing a mezuzah
Blessed are You, Lord our God, king of the universe, Who sanctifies us with His holy commandments And commands us to fix a mezuzah.

About this prayer

This blessing is said when a mezuzah is fixed to a doorpost. The mezuzah should be fixed to the right-hand side of the door, at a slight slant so that the top points inside the house. Some Jews kiss the mezuzah as they go into the house. In many Jewish homes, a mezuzah may be fixed to every door in the house, apart from the bathroom. The person fixing the mezuzah says the blessing, then everyone says 'Amen'.

A mezuzah fixed to a doorpost. Some Jews touch or kiss it as they enter the house.

their doors. A specially trained scribe writes out the passages by hand. Then the parchment is rolled up and placed inside the case. By fixing a mezuzah, God's words are constantly kept in the hearts and minds of the occupants.

Special Occasions

In Judaism, the key times in a person's life are marked by special ceremonies. Prayer brings God's presence to these celebrations and helps to give them meaning.

The birth of a baby

To mark the birth of a baby, there are ceremonies at home and in the synagogue. The Brit Milah ceremony takes place when a baby boy is eight days old. The baby is circumcised, as God commanded in the Torah. He is also given his name. By circumcising his son, a Jewish father enters him into the same convenant that God made with Abraham.

Father of all mankind, and source of all life, through Your great love I enter Your house to thank You and to bless Your name.
You have given me the joy of creation, which supported me in my weakness, and comforted me in my anxiety.
Your mercy has restored me. I thank You for my life and the life of my child, for You renew the wonder of creation.

About this prayer

There is no Brit Milah ceremony for a baby girl. Progressive Jews mark a girl's birth during a Shabbat service at the synagogue a few weeks later. The parents stand before the Ark and recite a prayer of thanksgiving like this one, which the mother would say. In Orthodox synagogues, at the next Shabbat service after a birth, prayers are said for the mother's well-being and the new baby's name is announced. The mother does not attend the service.

A Jewish couple with their baby.

Growing up

When a Jewish boy is 13, he starts his adult religious life. A Bar Mitzvah ceremony is held for him in the synagogue. Bar Mitzvah means 'Son of the Commandments'. The boy is called up to the Bimah to read from the Torah. Then he is blessed and reminded of his new duty to obey all the Jewish laws. Jewish girls are thought of as adults

↑ *A Progressive Jewish girl reads the Torah at her Bat Mitzvah.*

when they are 12 years old. To mark this, they have a ceremony called a Bat Mitzvah ('Daughter of the Commandments'). In some synagogues, girls read from the Torah. In others, they give a speech based on the teachings of the Torah.

In the presence of my teachers, the leaders and members of this holy congregation, I now prepare to take upon myself the duties which are binding on all the family of Israel. I ask their help in the years that lie ahead to strengthen my loyalty and devotion so that I may grow in charity and good deeds. I think also of those who have gone before me, who through all the troubles of the world preserved this heritage of holiness and goodness, so that I should enter into it now.

About this prayer
This is part of a prayer which a Progressive Jewish boy says at his Bar Mitzvah. He reads it out in English, often after the rabbi has spoken to him about his new duties. The boy states his commitment to the Jewish faith and community in public, witnessed by the rest of the congregation – including his family and friends – who are present at the ceremony.

Getting married

Jewish weddings usually take place in the synagogue. During the ceremony, the bride and groom stand under a canopy, called a huppah. It symbolises the new home that they will share. During the ceremony, the groom gives the bride a ring (the bride may also give one to the groom). A ring is a sign of their marriage but also represents a new link in a chain reaching back through many generations of Jews.

A Jewish wedding taking place under a huppah canopy.

Lord, at the quietness of this time, and in the holiness of this place, give Your blessing to Your children. You have given them youth with its hopes and love with its dreams. May these come true through their faith in each other and their trust in You. Let them be devoted to each other, and as the years go by, teach them how great is the joy that comes from sharing, and how deep the love that grows with giving. May Your presence dwell among them in the warmth of their love, in the kindness of their house, and in their charity for others.

About this prayer
The wedding ceremony is conducted by a rabbi who makes a speech about the couple and blesses them. This prayer is said by the rabbi in Progressive synagogues as the bride and groom stand under the huppah. It is said in Hebrew. Other prayers are also sung.

24

Death and mourning

When a Jewish person is dying, he or she tries to say the words of the Shema prayer (see page 18). This is a way of showing that the person accepts death as God's will. If this is not possible, other people should say the words. Special prayers are then said at the funeral service. These prayers include Kaddish (see right). After the funeral, there are seven days of mourning. Friends and relatives visit the family's house to offer prayers and sympathy.

Let us magnify and let us sanctify the great name of God in the world which He created according to His will. May His kingdom come in your lifetime, and in your days, and in the lifetime of the family of Israel - quickly and speedily may it come. Amen.

About this prayer

This is the beginning of the Kaddish prayer which mourners recite at a funeral. It is said in an ancient language called Aramaic which is close to Hebrew. The prayer is a great source of strength and comfort for the mourners. At a time of darkness and sorrow, they continue to feel God's holy presence and pray that God will be sanctified (held to be holy) by all of the world.

A candle is lit and prayers said on the anniversary of a person's death.

Festival Prayers

There are many Jewish festivals throughout the year. These are important occasions for prayer and worship. Most festivals remember key events from Jewish history and are thousands of years old. Each festival has its own ceremonies which take place in the synagogue and at home.

At Rosh Hashanah, a shofar (ram's horn) is blown to call Jews to observe the Ten Days of Penitence.

Ten holy days

The festival of Rosh Hashanah in September or October marks the start of the Ten Days of Penitence. These are the holiest days of the Jewish year. They are a solemn time when Jews look back at the past year and think about the good and bad things they have done.

Yom Kippur

The tenth day is called Yom Kippur (the Day of Atonement). This is when Jews atone (ask for God's forgiveness) for their sins and promise to live better lives in future. It is a day when Jews return to God. They leave their sins behind, thanks to God's grace and forgiveness. Everyone who can fasts and spends the whole day in the synagogue.

A Jewish man prays privately at a synagogue during the day-long Yom Kippur service.

*Hear our voice, Lord our God,
show us mercy and compassion,
accept our prayers willingly and
with love.
Turn us back to You, Lord,
And we shall return;
Renew our lives as of old.
Hear what we say; understand
What we cannot express.
May the words of our mouths
And the meditations of our hearts
Be acceptable to You,
O Lord, our rock and our
redeemer.*

About this prayer

This Yom Kippur prayer is one of the prayers for forgiveness recited during the services for the Ten Days of Penitence. It expresses the longing to turn away from our sins and wrong-doings, and to turn back to God through God's help and forgiveness. It is a prayer which Jews say together to show that they stand before God as a community. They share their joys and sorrows, take responsibility for each other and for all that they do in their lives.

Pilgrim festivals

Pesach, Shavuot and Sukkot are called the pilgrim festivals because they were occasions when, according to the Torah, Jews had to go to the Temple in Jerusalem. Pesach is celebrated in March or April. At this time, Jews remember how God helped their ancestors to escape from slavery in Egypt, and thank God for their freedom. Seven weeks later, Shavuot takes place. It celebrates how, after the Jews' escape, God gave the Torah to Moses on Mount Sinai. Sukkot recalls the fragile shelters that the Jews built on their journey from Egypt to the Promised Land.

↑ *A grandfather and his grandsons recite from the Haggadah during the Pesach meal.*

*Why is this night
Different from all other nights?*

*Because we were once slaves
Of the Pharaoh in Egypt;
But the Lord heard our voice;
He felt our sorrow
And understood our oppression;
With His powerful hand
And His outstretched arm
He led us out of Egypt.
Then we were at last set free.*

*Blessed is the Lord,
Who promised salvation to Israel:
He has kept His promise
And kept His Covenant He established with Abraham.*

About this passage

On the first night of Pesach, Jews gather at home to eat a special meal and tell the story of their escape from Egypt. They use a book called the Haggadah which means 'telling the story'. The youngest person present asks the storyteller questions about what happened, as in the passage above. The rest of the passage gives the answer. Reciting the story of Pesach is an act of praise and thanksgiving to God.

Hanukkah

Hanukkah, the festival of lights, is celebrated in November or December. It lasts for eight days and reminds Jews of a time long ago when the Jews won back the Temple in Jerusalem from enemies. The Jews had only enough oil left to keep the Temple lamp burning for one day. But, by a miracle, God kept the lamp burning for eight days until more oil could be found.

Lighting the Hanukkah candles.

These candles which now we light
Are in remembrance of the miracle of
our deliverance,
Of the wondrous and glorious deeds
That You performed for our fathers
of old
And still perform for us today
Through Your holy priests.
For the eight days of Hanukkah
These candles are holy,
And we cannot look at them
Without giving praise and honour to
You, O Lord,
For the wonders and miracles that
You have performed
And for Your glory.

About this prayer

During Hanukkah, Jews light candles on a special candleabra to remember the miracle that happened in the Temple. The eight candles stand for the eight nights that God kept the Temple lamp burning. (The ninth candle is used to light the others.) One candle is lit on the first night; two on the second; three on the third and so on until all eight are lit. This prayer is said immediately after the candles have been lit. The candles remind Jews of the dark times in their history when God was still present and their faith survived against the odds. They are a sign of faith and hope, and a source of support and reassurance.

Glossary

Anniversary The marking of a special date, such as someone's death, on the same day each year.

Ark The alcove, or cupboard, at the front of a synagogue which contains the Torah scrolls.

Bar Mitzvah This means 'Son of the Commandments'. A ceremony held when a Jewish boy is 13 and starts his adult religious life.

Bat Mitzvah This means 'Daughter of the Commandments'. A ceremony held when a Jewish girl is 12 and starts her adult religious life.

Brit Milah The ceremony at which a Jewish baby boy is circumcised.

Cantor A Jew trained to lead services in the synagogue, including singing prayers.

Circumcised When a Jewish baby boy has a small piece of skin cut from the end of his penis.

Covenant A special agreement made between God and the Jewish people.

Hebrew The ancient language of the Jews and of modern Israel.

Hebrew Bible Also called the Tenakh. The 24 books of the Hebrew Bible include the Torah (Books of Teaching), the Nevi'im (Books of the Prophets) and the Ketuvim (Books of Writings).

Jerusalem The city in Israel which is sacred to the Jews. It was the ancient capital of the Promised Land and is also the capital of modern Israel.

Kippah A cap or head covering worn during prayers. The plural is kippot.

Moses The Jewish leader who led the Jews out of slavery in Egypt and received the Torah from God on Mount Sinai.

Orthodox Holding traditional views. Orthodox Jews follow the traditions and laws of Judaism, many of which are over 2,000 years old.

Penitence A state of being sorry for things that you have done wrong.

Pilgrim A person who makes a journey (a pilgrimage) to a holy place.

Progressive Having forward-looking views. Progressive Jews believe that Judaism must adapt to suit modern times and concerns.

Psalms Songs of praise found in the Book of Psalms in the Hebrew Bible. They are very popular and important prayers in Judaism.

Rabbis Jewish religious teachers and leaders of Jewish communities.

Shofar A musical instrument made from a ram's horn which is blown on Rosh Hashanah and at the end of Yom Kippur. The sound is supposed to wake people up so that they can look at their lives and say sorry for any wrong doings.

Synagogue A Jewish place of worship, prayer, study and meeting.

Temple The ancient Jewish Temple in Jerusalem which was destroyed and rebuilt several times. Only one wall, called the Western Wall, was left standing. Jews from all over the world visit the Wall to pray.

Tenakh See Hebrew Bible. The word is made up of the initials of the three collections of books - T (Torah), N (Nevi'im) and K (Ketuvim).

Torah The Five Books of Teaching in the Hebrew Bible which include stories about the first Jews and more than 600 laws.

Further Information

Books to read
Sacred Texts: The Torah
Vivienne Cato, Evans Brothers 2003

Jewish Festivals Through the Year
Anita Ganeri, Franklin Watts 2003

Religion in Focus: Judaism
Geoff Teece, Franklin Watts 2003

Keystones: Jewish Synagogue
Laurie Rosenberg, A & C Black 2000

World Religions: Judaism
Angela Wood, Franklin Watts 1999

Websites
www.everythingjewish.com
A website packed with information about all aspects of Judaism.

www.judaism.about.com
Explores Jewish culture and religion.

www.jewfaq.org/prayer
A selection of Jewish prayers, with information about when and how they are said.

www.worldprayers.org
A collection of prayers from many different faiths and traditions.

Index